VOLLEYBALL

Learn in-depth knowledge about volleyball, rules, skills, tips and technique to excel in the sport against any opposing team.

VERONICA ASHLEY

TABLE OF CONTENTS

CHAPTER 1

INTRODUCTION

Volleyball is a team sport involving a net and a ball. On either side of the net are teams. When one team strikes the ball over the net and into the other team's court or area, the opposing team must return the ball over the net and into play within three attempts without allowing the ball to touch the ground. There are two primary types of competitive volleyball performed worldwide. There are competitive divisions for both indoor and beach volleyball, both of which are Olympic sports with competitive leagues. Volleyball is played on a hard court indoors with six players per team. Beach volleyball is played in the sand outdoors with two players per team. Volleyball strategy, regulations, and discussion will center on team volleyball. Anyone can pick up a ball and play with a group of friends; virtually anyone can participate in. To become a competitive player requires extensive practice. To play the game, you must have good height and jumping abilities.

THE ORIGINS OF VOLLEYBALL

Volleyball was created by William Morgan in 1885. He was the athletic director at the YMCA and created volleyball in an attempt to imitate basketball. Since then, the rules have undergone minor modifications, but the sport rapidly gained popularity at the YMCA. The term volleyball was coined by Alfred Halstead, who observed the game's volleying nature. People proclaimed it to be the name of volleyball, and it stuck. Volleyball was introduced to the Olympics for the first time in

1964. Japan earned the first gold medal in the women's volleyball category, while the USSR won the first gold in the men's volleyball category.

Let's take our concentration to the most popular form of volleyball; the indoor volleyball

Volleyball Ball

A volleyball used for indoor play is often white, but it can also be other colors. It typically has 8 or 16 panels and is constructed of leather. The official indoor volleyball ball is 25.5–26.5 inches in circumference and weighs 9.2–9.9 ounces. Air pressure in a typical ball ranges from 4.3 to 4.6 psi. A volleyball for youngsters is a little bit smaller. The balls used for beach volleyball are slightly larger, weigh the same, but have significantly less air pressure.

Volleyball Court Dimension

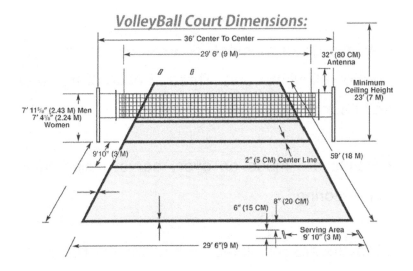

The volleyball court is 9 meters in width by 18 meters in length. The net splits it in half, creating sides. The net is 1 m wide and is positioned at a height of 7 feet, 11 5/8 inches (8 ft, approximately). The other important element is a line that is drawn 3 meters from the net and parallel to the net on each side. The attack line is this line. It designates the volleyball court's front row and back row areas.

CHAPTER 2

VOLLEYBALL RULES

• At any given moment, only six players may be on the volleyball court. Three in each of the front and back rows.

• Points are made on every serve, called rally-point scoring.

• Players are prohibited from hitting the ball twice in a row (a block is not regarded as a hit).

• A ball that touches the boundary line is deemed to be "in."

• A ball is 'out' if it contacts an antenna, any cables or net outside the antennae, the floor area entirely outside the court, the pole or referee stand, or the ceiling above a non-playable area.

• In this game, making contact with the ball with any part of the player's body is acceptable.

• Throwing, holding, or catching the ball is prohibited.

• Attacking or blocking a serve from inside or close to the 10-foot line is prohibited.

• Following the completion of the serve, the front-line players are free to shuffle their places at the net.

• The number of sets in a match depends on the difficulty of the game.

Player Positions

Both teams have six players. The players are divided into two groups of three in the frontcourt and three in the backcourt.

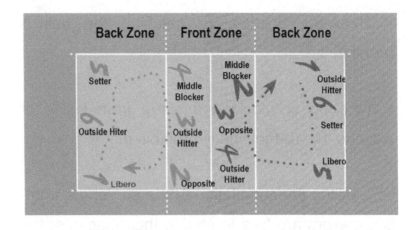

Player position and their Description

Setter: The primary responsibility of the setter is to position the ball so that the attackers can strike it with maximum force.

Middle Blocker: the primary blocker who occasionally engages in attack mode.

Outside Hitter: The principal attacker is positioned on the left and is prepared to spike.

Weakside Hitter: A secondary attacker whose primary duty is blocking who is occasionally prepared to spike when necessary.

Liberos: This person is referred regarded as the most crucial player because they are the center of the game. The first player to make contact with the ball is this one. They stand out from the rest of the squad since they don't wear the same jersey, and they can replace any player on the floor.

Terminologies in Volleyball

ACE: A serve that scores a point without allowing the recipient team to return it over the net.

BUMP: A pass is used to set an attack.

CARRY: This error happens when you hold a ball for an excessive amount of time.

CROSS: The middle attacker assumes the initiative of both attacking and defending in this style of play.

CUT: Shot from an impossible angle.

DIG: when the first pass is made after the first hit.

DOUBLE CONTACT: when a player strikes the ball twice in a row.

DUMP: when a player makes a second contact to cross the ball over the net.

FIVE ONE: A type of formation

FLOATER: A serving style in which the volleyball is hit without spin and with less force than usual, giving the impression that it is floating in the air.

FOUR TWO: A type of formation

JUMP SERVE: a serving technique in which the server throws the ball into the air before jumping up and striking the serve as it is falling.

KILL: an attack that successfully spikes as a result.

MISHIT: Untimed hit.

PANCAKE: Using the backhand flat to the ground, the player does a form of dig by letting the ball bounce off their hand during the stroke.

SIDE OUT: a change in serve brought on by a point loss.

SIX TWO: A six-player offense where there are two setters in the back row.

SPIKE: A type of attack in which the ball is served over the net with great force and speed.

STRONGSIDE: the left side of the court. given that the majority of the players are right-handed.

TIP: To quickly advance the ball over the net, a soft hit attack is used.

WEAKSIDE: The right side of the court. due to the fact that most of the players are right-handed.

WIPE: When a player pushes the volleyball off an opponent's block to win a point.

Volleyball Federation of India

In 1951, the Volleyball Federation of India, or VFI as it is more popularly known, was founded in India. The Indian Olympic Association (IOA) oversaw volleyball before the Indian Volleyball Federation (IVF) took over. From 1936 through 1950, the Interstate Championship (for men only) was held every two years. The first volleyball competition ever took place in Lahore in 1939. In 1951, the VFI conducted its inaugural meeting in Ludhiana, Punjab.

About V.F.I.

First President: Mr. F.C. Arora (1951–1954)

• Prof. Achyuta Samanta is the current president (2020–2024).

• Corporate office in Chennai, India

Fun Facts

The game was developed in Massachusetts around 1895. The invention of volleyball is credited to William G. Morgan.

• Volleyball was originally known as "mintonette," but that name was eventually altered. When G. Morgan learned that a spectator had noticed that the volleyball players were "volleying" the ball back and forth to each other over the net, the incident took place.

• The game was once played only inside.

In the 1930s, beach volleyball was invented in California.

• Beach volleyball with two players was first played in 1930.

• At the Paris Olympics in 1924, volleyball was played as an unauthorized game.

• At the 1964 Tokyo Olympics, men's and women's volleyball were made an official sport.

• When the Federation of International Volleyball (FIVB) was founded in 1947, volleyball became a recognized sport.

• In 1949, the first men's world championships were held. In contrast, the inaugural women's championship was held in 1952. At Will Rogers State Beach, the first professional beach volleyball competition was held in the summer of 1976. The "Olympic World Championship of Beach Volleyball" was the name of the competition.

• Beach volleyball was accepted as an Olympic sport in 1966, and participants often leap roughly 300 times in a single game.

- The only Olympic sport in which wearing too much is strictly forbidden is beach volleyball.

- The longest game ever played lasted for 75 hours and 30 minutes. North Carolina's Kingston hosted the game.

Volleyball regulations are created to ensure that the game runs efficiently, safely, and without giving any team an unfair advantage.

• The Court

Service Area

The region where the ball may be served is behind the endline and in between the extensions of the two sidelines.

Centerline

A line from sideline to sideline that parallels and passes immediately underneath the net. The two playing areas are divided by this line, which also designates the court's center. Rule of the middle:

Players may cross this line during play in American high school and USAV as long as they don't obstruct the opposition's ability to play the ball. In NCAA volleyball, players are permitted to walk entirely beyond the centerline as long as they don't obstruct play or put themselves in danger of getting hurt.

Attack Line

a line that separates the frontcourt from the backcourt on the court, 3 meters from and parallel to the net on each side. Attacking from the backcourt guidelines: Back-row players are not permitted to jump from in front of this line and assault the ball with their hands above the top of the net. The 3 meter line or 10 foot line are other names for the attack line.

Endline

The line that runs parallel to the net at the back of each playing area is known as the endline. The server must wait behind this line until serve contact is made when serving. The server can also choose to hop between servings. If your feet do leave the ground, like when performing a jump serve, they must do so from beyond the endline. The server can then land on the line or within the court after making contact with the ball.

Sidelines

The lines that delineate the court's sides are known as the sidelines. When the serve is made, all players must be in this area. Players are free to chase balls outside of these lines once the serve is made.

Frontcourt

The space between the attack line and the net is known as the frontcourt.

Backcourt

The space between the attack line and the finish line is known as the backcourt.

• Volleyball Equipment

The ball

Volleyball for Dummies tip: You can experiment with the use of punch balloons, beach balls, or rubber-bladed balls to introduce skills and change the learning environment during practices. Each player ought to have her own authorized volleyball in order to get a better feel for the ball's weight and feel.

The Net

Standards are poles to which the net is fastened. Three feet outside the playing field is where the standards are located. Whatever the format, you must routinely check all of the equipment for deterioration, loose or dangerous parts, and other flaws and replace or fix the volleyball equipment as necessary.

Knee Pads

Although it is legal to wear knee pads on grass or sand, they are commonly worn during games on hard surfaces to make it easier for players to accept landing on the ground. The foam or rubber that makes up knee pads is coated in a supple elastic material.

Clothing

The majority of practice and competition uniforms consist of just shorts and t-shirts. In a game, you can let your players wear whatever they like as long as it's loose enough to move freely and isn't restrictive. You should first check with your league before making any uniform decisions because some leagues mandate that teams wear coordinating shirts and shorts. Each uniform may also need to have numbers on it.

Learning Volleyball Basics

Setting, passing, spiking, serving, and other fundamental volleyball abilities are covered in the section on how to play volleyball. We also go over some of volleyball's most fundamental rules. Beginning volleyball players can study the most crucial facets of each technique in this area.

The volleyball skills area has additional in-depth information, such as the many volleyball passing techniques.

Various serve-receive techniques: "knee on the ground" technique on the right, high passing posture on the left, low passing position in the centre. For further details on fundamental volleyball skills, visit the volleyball skills section.

Rules for Playing Volleyball

We go over some very basic volleyball rules. Visit the volleyball fundamentals sections for extra information if you're seeking for more specifics.

Volleyball Match

In an indoor volleyball match, "the best out of five games" is typically used, which determines the winner based on who wins the first three games. Games at the junior varsity level might also be "the best of three," which means you must win two games to take the match. Typically, a volleyball game lasts until 25 points have been scored; however, certain leagues may employ 30-point games to decide the winner.

The fifth game, which serves as the decider, or the third game in a shorter match, is played until 15 points have been scored.

Two Point Difference in the End of the Games

"Two point difference" is required for the winning team to end the game – which means the game can continue longer than 15, 25 or 30 points.

After 15, 25, or 30 points, the game is won by the team that has a two-point advantage. In other words, the game can end 26-24, 27-25, 16-14, or 17-15; 25-24 or 15-14 are not viable outcomes.

How to Score a Point or Sideout

The winning team will receive a point. Every rally starts with a serve and finishes when one of the teams wins it. After either their own serve or the opponent's serve, a team may score a point.

Prior to the most recent rule modifications, a team could only score after its own serve. When a team won the rally following an opponent's serve, it was referred to as a sideout prior to the rule modifications. On volleyball courts, the phrase "sideout" is still used.

Volleyball Team

There are 6 volleyball players on the court.

Volleyball – Rotation

After each "sideout" (when the team wins the ball after the opponent serves), players rotate around the court, so a new person serves.

Front Row and Back Row Players

There are three players in the first row. The other three players are in the back row. The ball cannot be spiked, attacked, or blocked inside the 10-foot or 3-meter lines by back row players.

Libero

A player known as a libero wears a different color jersey. A defensive specialist known as a libero enters the game without a normal substitution. Any player on the back court can be replaced by the libero by going into the back court (typically the libero replaces the center or middle blocker). In international volleyball, the libero is not permitted to serve.

Substitutions

Libero movement on or off the court is not taken into account while calculating substitute. In international volleyball, substitutes are limited to a total of six per game. Take note that a few volleyball leagues in the USA permit limitless substitutions.

Volleyball – Game Flow

Rally and Scoring a Point

After winning a rally, a team receives a point. Volleyball serve initiates the rally. The player strikes the ball over the net between the antennae while positioned behind the backline.

How Many Hits Are Allowed in a Volleyball Game?

A volleyball team can play the ball into the opposing side of the net with a maximum of three hits.

In indoor volleyball, a block doesn't count as a touch, hence three hits are permitted after a block.

How to Winning a Rally

• A player kicks the ball into the opposing team's court (at least a portion of the ball must touch painted lines or stay inside painted lines).

• A player strikes the ball off an opponent.

• The opposing team can't get the ball back into your end.

• The opposing team kicks the ball off the line. The ball is deemed out of bounds if it strikes an antenna. In international volleyball, the ball is deemed out of bounds if it touches the ceiling. Some leagues permit play to continue even after the ball touches the ceiling.if a player makes a mistake or violates the rules while playing the ball. Visit the pages on the fundamental volleyball rules to gain more information about the mistakes and breaches.

VOLLEYBALL – SKILLS

Shuffling

Volleyball Players shuffle around the court as they move. When a player shuffling, they are taking several, very small steps backward, sideways, and forward without crossing their feet. You Can Play Volleyball Without Moving Around? WRONG!

Shuffling is a volleyball movement technique.

Have you ever overheard someone in gym class at school say, "Let's play volleyball because you don't have to move around and sweat in it."? It is a well-known fallacy regarding volleyball. It might surprise you to learn that volleyball players can move a few miles throughout a match.

Basic stance for volleyball

The fundamental posture is crucial for new volleyball players. When a volleyball player adopts a basic stance, their feet are slightly wider than their shoulders, their weight is front on their toes rather than their heels, their knees are bent, and their arms are free and in front of their bodies rather than intertwined.

What Are the First Volleyball Skills to Learn?

Players can start acquiring technical ball skills after mastering basic stance and shuffling.

How to Serve in Volleyball

Overhead or Underhand Serve?

A serve, whether it be an overhead or underhand serve, starts a volleyball rally.

Why to Serve Underhand?

Beginning volleyball players are advised to begin with an underhand serve.

The server finds it simpler, but more crucially, lengthier rallies are possible in practice. For new volleyball players, overhead serves can make serving and playing quite challenging. Although the serve's main function is to hinder the opponent's offense, it is not the greatest technique to teach new volleyball players.

Significant Underhand Serve Tips

It is not permitted to hold the ball in the hand when striking the serve; the player must toss the ball at least a little amount into the air.

Serving by Tossing the Ball Over

For the same reason, players may have thought about chucking the ball over the net instead of striking the serve early on.

Catch and Toss Volleyball Games

Younger volleyball players may be catching and tossing contacts in the early stages of play. For instance, the coach should insist that players only attempt to hit the ball over the net once they have made three contacts. The volleyball coach should progress toward actual volleyball matches gradually. The next phase is to only permit catch and toss with the initial contact, and the next step is to never allow catch and toss. The players frequently attempt to swing the ball with the third contact when playing these games. The coach should only permit bumping and setting with the third contact up until the spike and spike approach are introduced in order to ensure that rallies will go longer.

Allowing the offensive player to merely "spike approach + jump + tip" is a soft landing for hitting. The coach can approve "approach + jump + spike" for the players once they have mastered tipping.

Why catch and toss a ball?

Very young players can benefit by keeping the ball in the air for a longer period of time when catching and tossing. Additionally, it teaches players how to properly use three contacts when playing volleyball. Beginning volleyball players frequently keep hitting the ball over on the first contact when playing normal volleyball. They rapidly discover that throwing the ball as far to the other side as possible frequently produces the best results, which is bad for learning.

Volleyball Offense

The passing/serve/receive phase of volleyball offense is followed by setting and attacking (also known as spiking).

Passing

Passing, also known as the serve receive, happens after the opponent serves. Its function is to pass the ball to the setter, the team's playmaker.

Bumping or Overhead

Although volleyball players often pass the ball underhanded (by bumping), passing above (by setting) is now permitted as well.

How to Pass

When passing, the volleyball player adopts the standard stance, moves into position, stops, positions an arm platform beneath the ball, and strikes the ball with the smallest arm swing possible for the setting.

There is no need to swing the ball with your arms when receiving a serve.

When bumping a free ball, the body should provide additional power for the bump rather than just swinging the ball violently with the arms.

Serve Receivers / Passers

A libero, sometimes known as a defensive specialist, is a player who focuses on receiving and passing serves.

The outside hitter and the right side batter, who are all usually referred to as wings hitters, are typically also in charge of serving and receiving.

Volleyball Setting

After a serve, receive, or pass, the ball contacts the letter, which is a player. A set's objective is to position the ball for the attacking team. The setter makes a decision from a variety of possibilities in an effort to provide the team the best chance to score a point. Similar to a quarterback on a football team or a point guard on a basketball team is a setter.

Setting

Setting is typically done by raising the ball aloft with the fingers (hand setting), but occasionally it also needs to be done by passing the ball underhandedly to the attacker (bump setting).

How to Set

Hand Placement for Volleyball Setting

The player should place both hands above the brow when setting the ball with their fingers; their thumbs should make a triangle with their index fingers. The distance between the thumb and index finger should be between one and two inches. The player makes finger-to-finger contact with the ball rather of letting the ball touch the bottom of the hands.

Basic Volleyball Setting Footwork

The setter takes a left-right step as part of the fundamental setting footwork. Legs are somewhat bent because the right foot is about halfway between the left foot and the right foot, allowing the setter to push with their legs, especially when setting a longer distance. She then adjusts her weight forward after making contact with the ball, pushing forward with her legs and finishing with her left foot. Due to the weight transfer after the set, the left foot is in front of the right foot.

The rhytm "left-right-push through it" could be repeated by the setter to help them remember and understand the setting.

Volleyball Spiking / Attacking

It is advised not to spike the ball during practice sessions if you want to master the fundamentals of volleyball as quickly as possible because doing so shortens lengthy rallies.

It is advised to "set" or "bump" the ball over the net for beginner volleyball players to promote longer rallies.

How to Get Better at Volleyball Spike

Players can begin learning to spike by hitting the ball over the net with both feet on the ground at first as their skills advance and rallies grow longer.

Later, after refining the approach without the ball, players can attack by approaching, leaping into the air, and then tipping the ball into the opposing goal.

Players can begin spiking the ball over the net once they have learned the timing.

How to Spike

Approach

To gain speed, employ a four step method (first, take a right step, then a left step. Afterward, put both of your feet—right and left—on the ground so you can jump.)

OR, take a three-step technique (starting with a quick left step. Afterward, put both of your feet—right and left—on the ground so you can jump.)

Swing Your Arms to Raise Yourself

To lift yourself into the air, swing your arms vigorously.

It is crucial to practice without a ball for numerous training sessions to have the feet and the arms moving in unison.

Timing

A pretty accurate timing advice is to plant your first foot, either your right or left, on the ground as soon as the ball is released by the setter. This obviously depends on the set's speed, but it's a good generalization.

How to Attack on Offense in Volleyball

Where Do I Begin?

When speeding up, another good rule of thumb is to place your left foot midway between the 10-foot (3-meter) line and 2-feet off the 10-foot line. If you accelerate quickly, which is crucial for your vertical jump, it is close enough.

Spikers, Hitters, and Attackers

The opposite hitter is the player who focuses mostly on hitting. The position played by the opposite batter is that of the setter. The volleyball team's middle hitter (center, middle) and right side hitter (outside batters or wing hitters) both have attacking responsibilities.

Volleyball Defense

The goal of volleyball defense is to stop the other team's offensive from scoring. Blocking, digging, and coverage are all seen as forms of defense in volleyball. (In actuality, the coverage can be both because it is an essential component of offense as well.)

Blocking in volleyball

A volleyball block is an effort to stop an assault from the opposition.

How Can I Block?

To achieve this, jump up into the air slightly behind the assailant, push your hands over the net, and reach into the other side of the net in the direction of the assailant.

When blocking, keep your eyes wide open! Don't shut them!

Fundamental Volleyball Blocking Rules

In indoor volleyball, it doesn't count as a touch if the block makes contact with the ball. (A block counts as a touch in beach volleyball.)

Blocking is limited to three front row players who are positioned at the net.

Only after the third opponent contact can a blocker cross the net and enter the other side of the court to stop the ball. (Blockers are unable to prevent the setter from setting the ball.)

Both sides have the right to play the ball when it is in the plane of the net (i.e., when any portion of the ball is above the net). (Really, this is accurate! Even many refs struggle with this!). One more time: both teams can play the ball if it passes the net, even by a half-inch.

Volleyball Digging

Digging is an action used to try to stop the ball from falling into the court following an opponent attack. You can achieve that by burrowing with your fingers aloft or underhandedly (bump).

Three players in the rear row are primarily in charge of digging. The front row player's responsibility is to aid the back court players in defense if he doesn't block.

Defense in volleyball is crucial!

The most crucial aspect of digging is that defensive players and blockers must adhere to the defense strategy of the team (e.g., do they block the line or angle shots).

To adhere to the team's strategy, the players must have faith in one another. For instance, the defensive player just needs to be on the line to dig the ball if the blockers trust him or her to block the angle and dig the line shot. Otherwise, guesswork would be unending. Follow the defensive plan because the blocker might opt to block the line anyhow the next time because the defender wasn't there the last time!

Volleyball Coverage / Cover

Coverage is a defensive move in which players position themselves beneath the block in order to keep the ball in play in the event that the blocker blocks the hitter. The spiker may also purposefully swing towards the block and then use the block to deflect the ball back toward his or her own court. In order to dig the ball for the setter, the spiker needs teammates who are covering.

CHAPTER 3

TIPS FOR BEGINNERS IN VOLLEYBALL

Any sport requires knowledge of the techniques, regulations, and protocol. Each of these also develops with practice. Additionally, there are the minor details that you learn after playing for a long; these are things that unquestionably come with expertise. These 16 pointers, which you won't find in the volleyball rulebook, can help you score more points and improve your teamwork.

1. Call mine, even if it seems obvious

Calling mine when you're in position to take the volleyball is one of the first volleyball lessons you learn in elementary school. As you progress in volleyball, this habit develops, and even when it seems quite apparent, you always call mine. This inclination isn't as intuitive for novice players. Of course you'll get the ball if it's headed your way! However, some players may assume that the ball is still up for grabs and that someone needs to collect it if they don't hear someone calling "mine"!

Calling something "mine" may seem funny at first, but after participating in a few games, you'll notice how typical it really is. So don't be hesitant to ask for that ball and speak out!

2. Attempt to utilize all three hits.

Prior to sending the ball back over the net in volleyball, each team has three touches with the ball. (Well, technically, if one of those touches was a block, they receive 4 hits.) However, occasionally less skilled players may become anxious or scared by the ball and send the ball over the net before their team has utilized all three of its hits. Strategically, this can mean that a chance to score is lost. The traditional bump-set-spike play must be completed with all three hits. Therefore, if a player is using unneeded hits to push the ball past the goal, they may be passing up a chance to score.

That being said, occasionally striking the ball on the second hit can be its own strategy and lead to a point. What I'm trying to say is that players should consider when to shoot the ball over the goal to give their team the best chance at scoring, which frequently means using all three hits.

3. Avoid touching the second ball unless the setter has requested assistance.

In light of the three touches rule, this is a good moment to urge players to allow the setter to receive the second ball. A specialized position, the setter receives the second ball and positions the batters. The setter may need to sprint down the initial bump if it is off-target from where it should be going. And occasionally, that ball might be directly in the direction of another player. The setter is a specialized player whose job it is to set up the hitters, despite the temptation to just set the ball.

The issue about setters is that they are frequently QUICK! They will undoubtedly reach that second ball since it is what they have been taught to do. They'll almost certainly be able to get a good set to one of the hitters even if they're sprinting to the ball. They have also been taught when it makes more sense to allow a teammate take the second ball; in certain situations, they will indicate for a teammate to step in and set by calling out "help". Therefore, if the ball appears to be headed directly towards you, just keep an ear out for the setter's call for assistance, then move in and assist your partner!

4. Avoid placing the ball too close to the net.

One of the most frequent mistakes non-setter players make when the setter requests for help is setting the ball too close to the net. As a result, the hitter's hitting options are more constrained and they are unable to use their entire hitting strategy. A set that is too close to the net can be challenging to hit and potentially dangerous, particularly for blocks or hitters with less expertise. A hitter who isn't accustomed to reacting to a tight set can land in or under the net, possibly on the blockers' feet. This is one of the most typical volleyball injury scenarios, frequently leading to ankle or knee injuries. Aim approximately a foot away from the net rather than directly toward it. This provides some buffer space, even if it is somewhat off target. The hitter should be prepared to adjust as they shouldn't be anticipating a flawless set from a non-setter player in the first place.

5. Never touch down on or within the net.

It can be quite tempting to hit as many spikes as you can because, as a beginner player, you might not be earning as many sets. This is a terrific attitude, but be sure to keep your striking technique under control and to have a keen sense of where you are in relation to the net, especially the space beneath it. Players frequently fail to notice how near they are to the goal because they are so intent on hitting the ball. Keep in mind that touching the net is against the rules and might lose your side a point. The safety component, though, is even more crucial. There is a considerable probability that you will step on someone else's foot if you land in the net or underneath the net.

So, resist the urge to focus just on hitting the ball and train your spatial awareness to be aware of how near you are to the net.

6. Avoid passing the ball too near the net.

Passing (or bumping) the ball too closely to the goal is another common mistake. An over bump may be used to describe this. It is quite challenging for the setter to set the ball after an over bump, and even if they manage to obtain a set, they probably won't be able to run any plays. You can unintentionally be setting up the opposing team if you bump too close to the net. If a player from the opposing team happens to be in the perfect spot, they could just be able to timing a really beautiful hit when an over bump truly does go OVER the net. Obviously for their team. When passing the ball, try to aim about a foot or so from the net to prevent over bumps. The setter now has some space. And you, the passer, have some latitude in your aim.

7. Avoid catching the ball when it's in play.

This one seems ridiculous, I guess. Anyone familiar with volleyball regulations is aware that catching the ball is against the rules. But if you've ever attended a volleyball match, particularly a tournament, you know how loud it can get. Players are shouting, shoes are squeaking on the gym floor, volleyballs are bouncing, and whistles are being blown by officials on various courts. It's simple for a player to THINK they heard the whistle sound amid all the excitement and capture the ball to stop the play. However, if you are even the slightest bit uncertain as to whether you heard the whistle blow or not, CONTINUE PLAYING! I assure you that catching the ball during an active play would make you appear much more dumb than continuing the game after the whistle has been blown! The play will eventually come to an end because the players will either figure it out or the referee will blow their whistle once more.

8. Always pack the necessary equipment, as well as perhaps some more.

Yes, it's simple to occasionally forget to bring something. even the best of us experience this. However, avoid allowing it to occur frequently. Use a checklist or pack your bag when you aren't pressed for time so you can check to be sure you have everything you need. There are some things you can borrow, like fresh shorts and socks. Additionally, there are some items that you probably don't want to share, such as a sweat towel or a water bottle.

9. Organize your tools!

Regarding equipment, be sure to clean it frequently. You'll wash your athletic attire, of course. I'm referring to your ankle braces and knee protection, though. Don't just toss them in your bag after a game until the following week's game. As soon as they require it, wash them and give them a chance to air out. Although YOU might not notice it, volleyball equipment might smell HORRIBLE if you don't like it.

10. Wear the appropriate clothing.

It's typical to not have all the equipment when you first start a new sport. Before investing in potentially pricey gear, you should be sure you genuinely enjoy the sport. However, there are a few things to remember when it comes to volleyball equipment that most likely won't set you back any more cash.

Due to the fact that volleyball is a court sport, you should wear indoor shoes. Make sure you're not wearing outdoor shoes on the court, even if you're not buying specific volleyball shoes right away. Any mud or water that is tracked onto the field of play poses a risk since it might make players trip as they race for the ball. Instead of looking at the ground, they will be gazing up at the ball.

To avoid leaving skid marks on the gym floor, indoor footwear should also be non-marking.

Although they are not required, knee pads can occasionally offer rookie players a little bit more confidence when diving for the ball. Just keep in mind that effective diving technique actually doesn't entail getting on your knees to bump; rather, you should be moving further forward. Volleyball players typically don more fitting gym attire rather than baggy attire. This happens frequently because even if only your clothes touched the net, you could still be penalized for a net infringement. Although you don't have to dress entirely in spandex, consider choosing gym attire that is more fitting than baggy.

11. Don't just jump straight up when blocking

Many people believe that preventing a spike involves simply jumping straight up with your arms in the air. At the peak of your jump, you should actually thrust your hands forward to simulate pushing against the volleyball as it is being spiked. Your block will be significantly stronger as a result of this push, which should stop the ball's velocity from simply pushing through your hands. Just be careful to jump high enough over the net to push over the height of the net and avoid touching it at all, otherwise you run the danger of receiving a net violation call.

12. When serving, avoid receiving a foot violation.

You can only begin a play with full control of the ball when you are serving. Considering that each player is allowed to choose how much space they require for their serve, you would believe that no one would ever receive a foot violation. Even though it rarely occurs, getting a foot violation while serving is somewhat embarrassing. Furthermore, it can happen to skilled players as well; they might mistake where they are as they begin their serve. But regardless of how long you've been playing, it's always a real "d'oh" moment when you hear the whistle sound for a foot infraction.

The simplest approach to prevent receiving this humiliating call is to always scan the lines as you return to duty and ensure that you are beginning back far enough to allow for the necessary space. Additionally, you may want to practice your serve outside of a game setting so that you can determine how much space you need to serve and become extremely accustomed to it.

13. Ascertain that you are in a defensive position.

When the opposing side is preparing to set up an attack and spike the ball over, you take a defensive stance. If you are in a strong defensive position, you can fend off the attack as soon as feasible. It is not a defensive position to stand with your legs straight and your arms clasped in front of you. This is a place to watch from. When a player is in a good defensive posture, their arms are bent in front of them, allowing them to move swiftly in any direction to react to the ball's movement. The player's legs are bowed, his waist is bent forward, and he is leaning slightly forward. The phrase "on your toes" originated from this forward lean. More than just being able to physically react to the ball is required to be in a strong defensive position. It involves anticipating where the ball will go and being psychologically prepared to react. A player who is in a good defensive position is aware that the ball may come their way and is prepared to react to it.

14. Be prepared for the ball at all times.

With 6 players on the court and only 3 touches allowed per play, this implies that at least 3 players must miss their chance to touch the ball before it crosses the goal line for each play. Be sure to play if you're one of the six players on the court and avoid being seen watching. You never know when a terrible pass will need to be ran down, when a player who doesn't set the ball will have to do so, or which hitter will get the set.

Back-court players who are not prepared to get a set are one of the most frequent players who are not ready for the ball. A backcourt player may receive a set as a result of a poor pass or on purpose to diversify the assault. Therefore, keep in mind that back-court players can still get a set even while they are there! Even if it seems like you won't be in the play, always be prepared.

15. Ensure that you warm up.

Recreational league players frequently arrive late for a game, hustle to tie their shoes, and then simply run onto the court without any form of warmup. There is no way that putting on your indoor shoes qualifies as a warmup. In order to improve performance and reduce injury risk, a solid warmup gets the muscles and ligaments ready for the more demanding use that will come with the physical activity.

Ironically, you actually NEED to warm up more as you age. Lack of a proper warmup makes muscles, joints, and ligaments more prone to injury because they may not be as flexible as they once were. It's never a nice thing to get hurt. It can not only keep you from participating in your favorite sports and hobbies, but it can also keep you from carrying out your daily obligations Additionally, studies have revealed that senior athletes may require more time to recover from injuries than younger competitors.

Therefore, give yourself a thorough warm-up to get ready for the game. Consider the time needed for a warmup as merely a portion of the overall time needed for the activity. This is a smart practice. If the game starts at 7:30, for instance, get at the gym no later than 7:00 to give yourself plenty of time to put on your gear and warm up.

16. Don't forget to cool off as well!

Even while it may be tempting to go out for drinks soon after the game, a proper cool down is just as crucial as a proper warmup. Doing some good stretches now, when your muscles and ligaments are warm, will stop the lactic acid from building up and help prevent pain. It's not necessary to have a difficult cool down. Include only a few essential stretches, paying particular attention to the muscles you used most throughout the game. You may also utilize this opportunity to joke around with your teammates about any of them who received a foot violation when serving the ball as well as discuss how the game went.

When you next step onto the volleyball court, keep these suggestions in mind. Even if you haven't played volleyball for a long time, these pointers will make you feel more at ease on the court.

CHAPTER 4

THE 5 MOST POPULAR FORMS OF VOLLEYBALL

Volleyball is believed to be one of the 10 most popular sports in the globe. With over 900 million estimated admirers and a lengthy history, volleyball's diversification was inevitable. Since its inception, the game has developed in a variety of methods. Occasionally, players adapted new rules, new strategies, and sometimes they simply reinvented the game by inventing new methods to play. Regardless of how we arrived at this point, human creativity has produced numerous variants of this wonderful sport.

In order of worldwide popularity, the five most popular volleyball variations are:

1. Indoor Volleyball

2. Beach Volleyball

3. Kick Volleyball (Sepak Takraw)

4. Footvolley

5. Snow Volleyball

This list will take us around the globe to discover the inventiveness behind all of these variants.

1. Indoor Volleyball

Overview

Indoor volleyball is the common term for the classic form of volleyball that we know and enjoy today. YMCA physical director William G. Morgan allegedly devised the sport in 1895 in Holyoke, Massachusetts. This form of volleyball is traditionally played in gymnasiums on a large court with a net in the center. The game is played through a series of rallies in which two teams vie for a point. The set is won by the first team to win 25 points/rallies. A team begins a rally by serving the ball to the opposing team. To score a point, players will endeavor to place the ball on the opposite side of the court from their opponent.

They are permitted to use any portion of their body to make contact with the ball, although hands are the most common. In addition, the rules prohibit them from holding the ball in any manner. Before the ball must be returned to the opposing side of the net, each team is permitted a maximum of three touches.

Court Size	59 feet (18.29 meters) long by 29.5 feet (9 meters) wide.
Number of players	Teams must have 6 players on the court during play.
Net Height	Men's: The net is 2.43 m (7 ft 11 in) Women's: The net is 2.24 m (7 ft 4 in).

The Ball

Depending on age, gender, and skill level, the volleyball's characteristics can vary. Typically, competitors employ a ball with a circumference of 25.5-26.5 inches and an internal pressure of 4.24-4.61 psi. The weight of the ball is between 9.2 and 9.9 ounces. See below for an illustration of an indoor volleyball.

This Mikasa V200W volleyball is presently the official FIVB game ball for the 2020 (now 2021) Tokyo Olympic Games.

Competition

Indoor volleyball, the original format of the sport, features the greatest variety of competitions among all volleyball formats. There are numerous competitive divisions at which athletes can compete. This includes schools, organizations, and colleges, as well as professional volleyball and international tournaments. Since the 1964 Tokyo Olympic Games, volleyball has also been a feature of the Summer Olympics.

Popularity

Indoor volleyball is ranked first on this list due to the fact that it is the original and most popular form of the sport. The FIVB is the greatest international sports governing body, with 221 member Federations. They estimate that over 800 million athletes worldwide participate in volleyball. The FIVB is responsible for organizing international tournaments, adopting and enhancing rules of play, and instructing and certifying referees and coaches. In addition, they are leaders in the global promotion of the sport.

2. Beach Volleyball

Overview

Beach volleyball is without question the most prevalent variant of volleyball. It is believed to have originated in Hawaii approximately in 1915. As its name suggests, beach volleyball is an adaptation of volleyball played on sandy beaches rather than indoors. Similar to indoor volleyball, this variation pits two teams against each other on a court with the objective of landing the ball on the opposing side. Despite the variant's modifications, the primary mechanics and gameplay remain firmly rooted in the original volleyball format.

Variations and Distinctions

In addition to rule modifications, the game features a distinct court size, number of players, and ball. Additionally, beach volleyball incorporates the outdoors. The weather can have a significant impact on the gameplay. Rain, wind, and sunlight can all have an impact on the game.

Here are some additional important distinctions:

• The required quantity of points to win decreases from 25 to 21.

• Open-handed tips and dinks are prohibited.

• As opposed to indoor volleyball, the block touch will contribute towards the maximum of three touches.

• Each player does not have a designated position.

• Beach volleyball teams swap sides of the court every seven points to ensure fairness and mitigate the impact of weather. This ensures that no team has an environmental advantage, such as wind or sun radiation.

• The court is constructed entirely of sand.

Court Size	52.5 feet (16 meters) long by 26.2 feet (8 meters) wide.
Number of players	2 players per team.
Net Height	Men's: The net is 2.43 m (7 ft 11 in). Women's: The net is 2.24 m (7 ft 4 in).

3. Kick Volleyball (Sepak Takraw)

Overview

Kick volleyball, also known as sepak takraw, is a competitive sport that consists of two teams of three players, the left inside, right inside, and back. The court where the game is played has a net that is 1.5 meters height and is roughly the same size as a badminton court. Although current versions are often synthetic, the grapefruit-sized balls are originally weaved from bamboo or rattan.

The Ball

The Sepak Takraw ball is spherical and constructed of synthetic fiber or a woven layer. Originally, a rattan ball was used, but the availability of newer technologies and materials prompted a transition to synthetic fiber and rubberized plastic.

According to the rules, the ball must contain 12 holes and 20 intersections. The circumference should be between 16.14 and 17.3 inches (0.41 and 0.44 meters). For men, the ball should weigh between 170g and 180g, and for women, between 150g and 160g.

Competition

Similar to indoor volleyball, this game features multiple categories of competition. The King's Cup Sepaktakraw World Championship is the most prestigious Sepak Takraw competition. The Asian Sepaktakraw Federation (ASTAF) was established in 1965 to regulate the sport in Asia, and the International Sepaktakraw Federation (ISTAF) was established in 1992 as the world governing body for the sport. Because the game is so entrenched in Southeast Asian countries, few western teams will qualify for this competition. In fact, Thailand, Vietnam, Malaysia, Indonesia, and other countries in the region will be represented and win this form of competition.

Regarding other levels of competition, little is known, although numerous schools and organizations compete in many southeast Asian nations.

Popularity

Although Sepak Takraw is not an Olympic sport, the game remains immensely popular in its native region. In fact, Sepak Takraw is the most popular sport at the Asian Games, the world's second-largest multi-sport competition after the Olympics.

I wish I could provide you with some statistics, but it is extremely difficult to collect information and data on the prevalence of Sepak Takraw. My standard response to this type of situation is to check YouTube and see how popular videos on the subject are. Sepak Takraw appears to be performing very well based on this metric and effortlessly earns the third position on this list.

For most non-Asian nations, it is difficult to comprehend the magnitude of this game. The game is an integral element of Southeast Asian culture. Throughout Southeast Asia, it is common to find Sepak Takraw courts in schools and parks, while many children also play in the fields and on the roadways.

4. Footvolley

Overview

It was a certainty. The most popular sport in the world had to be involved. Footvolley is a combination of beach volleyball and soccer. In this variation of volleyball, players are prohibited from using their hands and play with a soccer ball while adhering to many beach volleyball regulations. Footvolley may sound comparable to our preceding volleyball variant, but it is in fact a completely distinct form of volleyball. In the 1960s, this variation originated in Brazil. The rumor states that the game was conceived at a time when soccer was prohibited on many public beaches but beach volleyball courts were still accessible. The soccer players were required to adapt and innovate on this new field.

Variations and Distinctions

As stated previously, there aren't that many rules and variations, but the ones that do exist drastically alter the game.

Here are the alterations:

Players are prohibited from using their arms and hands.

• The ball is substituted with one resembling a soccer ball.

• Players are permitted multiple consecutive touches with the ball.

• Most games consist of a single set to 18 points.

• Games in competitions can be best-of-three,

Court Size	Depending on the setting, the court will be: – 52.5 feet (16 meters) long by 26.2 feet (8 meters) wide. (same as beach volleyball) – 59 feet (18.29 meters) long by 29.5 feet (9 meters) wide. (same as indoor volleyball)
Number of players	2 players per team.
Net Height	Men's: The net should be set at 2.15 m (7 in). Women's: The net should be set at 2 m (6 ft 6 in).

with 15 points required to win a set.

The Ball

Footvolley uses a ball that is the same size as a volleyball and has components that closely resemble soccer balls. Hard synthetic leather is used to make the balls. All official game balls, like the one below, are created with materials and production practices that have been approved by FIFA.

Competition

In South America, Europe, and the US, the sport is fairly active. The Pro Footvolley Tour has been held annually in America since 2008. Media outlets including ESPN, AT&T Sports, Spectrum Sports, and many others have covered the event. Similar to how South America hosts numerous leagues, contests, and other events, Europe hosts the European Footvolley League. The

Futevôlei (Footvolley) World Cup is the premier competition in the sport, and it is generally always hosted by a South American nation, however it is not unique to South America.

Popularity

The popularity of footvolley is growing and will continue to grow. It should come as no surprise that people would enjoy this game given how popular soccer is throughout the world. Without a doubt, soccer is the most popular sport in the world. Because of this, followers of both sports are likely to find a variation like Footvolley appealing. It makes sense that Footvolley started in South America because soccer is essentially a religion for many people. According to my perception, the game is so popular there that it is impossible to predict which game will be played on the beach volleyball court when you visit the beach.

5. Snow Volleyball

Overview

The last and last entry is Snow Volleyball. Snow volleyball first appeared in Europe in the early 1900s, and it has since gained popularity in places like Russia, Austria, and Switzerland. The sport didn't really take off until the first Snow Volleyball Tour in Wagrain, Austria, in 2008. Since then, the sport has grown to include matches in several European nations, culminating in 2019 with the start of the FIVB Snow Volleyball World Tour. Plans and debates supporting the inclusion of snow volleyball in future winter Olympic games are ongoing. The FIVB's lineup of volleyball variations now includes this most recent addition. With a few minor alterations, the essential rules and gameplay of this format are very similar to those of indoor and beach volleyball.

Variations and distinctions

Many beach volleyball varieties are adopted by snow volleyball, and some of them are modified for the snowy climate. The following are the variations from snow volleyball:

• Similar to indoor volleyball, the block touch will not count toward the 3 touches permitted, reducing the required amount of points to win from 25 to 15.

• Open-handed tips and dinks are prohibited.

• Each team is permitted one substitute.

• The entire playing surface is snow.

• Another distinction is that, despite the lack of dress codes, players frequently compete in thermal apparel and some kind of snow-gripping footwear, such as cleats.

Court Size	52.5 feet (16 meters) long by 26.2 feet (8 meters) wide.
Number of players	3 players per team.
Net Height	Men's: The net should be set at 2.43 m (7 ft 11 in) Women's: The net should be set at 2.24 m (7 ft 4 in).

The Ball

Snow volleyballs are spherical and fashioned of a flexible, water-resistant plastic, just like beach volleyball. To better accommodate the chilly weather, the panels have been modified to have more cushioning and be softer.

Competition

There aren't many organized snow volleyball tournaments as of 2021. The FIVB and the European Volleyball Confederation are constantly thinking about how to grow the sport and will be holding more and more tournaments in the future.

Popularity

One of the most recent additions to the volleyball world is snow volleyball. Although it appears to be a highly successful and well-known game in northern European countries, there is still much to learn about the growth and popularity of this sport. I will personally keep a look out for this variation because it seems like a good addition to the volleyball world and I do live somewhere that gets a lot of snow every year.

THE END

Made in the USA
Monee, IL
26 September 2023